29   CU

C0-DAT-807

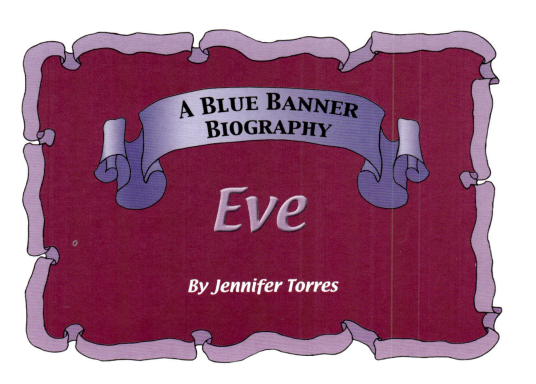

A BLUE BANNER BIOGRAPHY

Eve

By Jennifer Torres

Mitchell Lane
PUBLISHERS

P.O. Box 196
Hockessin, Delaware 19707
Visit us on the web: www.mitchelllane.com
Comments? email us: mitchelllane@mitchelllane.com

Copyright © 2005 by Mitchell Lane Publishers. All rights reserved. No part of this book may be reproduced without written permission from the publisher. Printed and bound in the United States of America.

Printing   1   2   3   4   5   6   7   8   9

Blue Banner Biographies

Alicia Keys	Allen Iverson	Avril Lavigne
Beyoncé	Bow Wow	Britney Spears
Christina Aguilera	Christopher Paul Curtis	Clay Aiken
Condoleezza Rice	Daniel Radcliffe	Derek Jeter
Eminem	**Eve**	Ja Rule
Jay-Z	Jennifer Lopez	J. K. Rowling
Jodie Foster	Lance Armstrong	Mary-Kate and Ashley Olsen
Melissa Gilbert	Michael Jackson	Missy Elliott
Nelly	P. Diddy	Queen Latifah
Rita Williams-Garcia	Ritchie Valens	Ron Howard
Rudy Giuliani	Sally Field	Selena
Shirley Temple		

Library of Congress Cataloging-in-Publication Data
Torres, Jennifer.
    Eve / Jennifer Torres.
        p. cm — (A blue banner biography)
    Includes bibliographical references and index.
    Discography: p.
    Filmography: p.
    ISBN 1-58415-317-2 (library bound)
    1. Eve (Musician) — Juvenile literature. 2. Rap musicians — United States — Biography — Juvenile
literature. I. Title. II. Series.
ML3930.E86T67 2004
782.421649'092 — dc22
                                                                                    2004021882

ABOUT THE AUTHOR: Jennifer Torres is a freelance writer and newspaper columnist based in Central Florida. Her articles have appeared in newspapers, parenting journals, and women's magazines across the country and Canada. When she's not writing she enjoys spending time at the beach with her husband John and their five children, Timothy, Emily, Isabelle, Daniel and Jacqueline.

PHOTO CREDITS: Cover—Evan Agostini/Getty Images; p. 4—Matthew Peyton/Getty Images; pp. 8, 27—Shooting Star; p. 12—Evan Agostini/Getty Images; p. 16—Scott Gries/Getty Images; p. 20—Kevin Winter/Getty Images; p. 25—George De Sota/Getty Images.

ACKNOWLEDGMENTS: The following story has been thoroughly researched, and to the best of our knowledge, represents a true story. While every possible effort has been made to ensure accuracy, the publisher will not assume liability for damages caused by inaccuracies in the data, and makes no warranty on the accuracy of the information contained herein. This story has not been authorized nor endorsed by Eve.

CONTENTS

Eve goes for the glamorous look as she smiles for the camera.

Grammy Winner

*T*he night was filled with stars. They were everywhere. As Eve walked down the red carpet to the 44th Annual Grammy Awards, passing singers like Alicia Keys and Usher, she knew she was with the best of the best. The girl from the Philadelphia ghetto had made the big-time. Everywhere she looked, there was an artist she had grown up watching on MTV or listening to on the radio.

It was February 27, 2002, and that night Eve would find out if she had won a Grammy Award. A Grammy is the top prize a musician can get. One of the two Grammys for which Eve had been nominated was a new award at that year's show. It was for the hit "Let Me Blow Ya Mind," a song she had done with Gwen Stefani, lead singer of the rock band No Doubt.

This was a very special night. Everyone was so dressed up. Some of the women wore long gowns and high heels. Eve wore a purple, red, and orange half-dress with black shorts. The outfit showed off her free spirit. She had a style all her own.

It was a big moment in the young rapper's life, but Eve wasn't about to get a big head. For Eve, the most important thing a person can do is "keep it real." To her that means always being honest with herself and others—and never forgetting where she came from. Still, the red carpet was a long way from home for the girl who had to work hard and scratch her way to the top.

Raised in the tough Philadelphia projects, Eve's childhood was a lesson in survival, but her dream of being a rap star helped her battle through the hard times.

Now that she was a celebrity, her hometown provided a special place where she could just be herself with family and old friends. They would be cheering for her on this night of nights.

> For Eve, the most important thing a person can do is "keep it real." To her that means always being honest with herself and others.

Eve never hangs around a lot of people, especially, she says, other stars. According to Eve, "Most of them are not real."

"I have to always remind myself that I cannot let all of this get to me. I see people every day in this business that have gotten caught up," she says. "It's bigger than this."

As Eve walked through the door of the Los Angeles Staples Center, the place where the Grammy Awards ceremony was being held, she was in awe. This was where artists she had grown up listening to—like Queen Latifah, LL Cool J, Ice-T, and Dr. Dre—had won Grammy Awards in years past. Now, she was right there with them. And the fans? They were cheering for her and calling out her name.

> *It really didn't matter if she won a grammy or not, just being there was an honor.*

It really didn't matter if she won a Grammy or not. Just being there was an honor. But later when the winner was called, Eve heard her name. She had won! It was a perfect night.

Eve's ride to the top was filled with bumps and curves but she never gave up her dream.

Humble Beginnings

*E*ve Jihan Jeffers was born November 10, 1978, in Philadelphia, Pennsylvania. She grew up in a two-bedroom apartment in the city's Mill Creek housing project. Money was tight.

Eve's mother, Julie Wilch, worked two jobs just to make ends meet. When she wasn't working, she was in school taking classes at the local college. The busy days left her very tired and with little time to spend with Eve.

Jerry Jeffers, Eve's father, was also very busy, but he tried to spend time with Eve now and then. When Eve was 12, her dad moved to North Carolina. Sometimes she was able to visit him there over the summers.

To Eve, though, it was her mom who shaped her life.

"I never looked up to any stars or anything when I was young," she says. "My mother was who I looked up to, because she was a strong, young black woman taking care of her business and her family."

> "I never looked up to any stars or anything when I was young. My mother was who I looked up to."

Eve spent a great deal of time alone. It made her independent. She fixed her own meals, washed laundry, and cleaned the house when her mom had to work late.

From a very early age, Eve was a ham. She loved to sing and dance around the house when she was alone. After a while she got up the nerve to invite friends over to watch her perform. Soon Eve was putting on a show for anyone who asked. She loved the feeling she got from it. That's when she knew the desire to perform was in her blood.

At the age of 11, Eve heard a new sound — rap. With three classmates, she began a group called Dope Girl Posse. Her friends in the group shared Eve's desire to entertain. You could find the girls any place there was a crowd, from the schoolyard to the local mall. Dope Girl Posse often took people by surprise by breaking out into song anywhere they found people to listen.

And rapping and dancing weren't the only ways they showed off. The group liked to dress in a style that got them noticed. Sometimes they wore sparkly shorts or neon tops. They entered talent shows and tried very hard to get discovered. They had dreams of fame.

The girls thought they would always be together. But one day everything changed. Eve's mother fell in love and remarried. Soon Eve had a baby half brother, named Farrod. Now instead of two, there were four in the family. They needed a bigger place to live. They moved to a home in

Her new home did not make Eve happy. Her friends were far away. Everything she knew was gone.

Philadelphia's Germantown neighborhood. While it was a good move in a lot of ways, it was not a good one for Eve's young dreams of stardom.

As a young girl, Eve learned to have her own sense of style and to believe in herself.

Her new home did not make Eve happy. Her friends were far away. Everything she knew was gone.

Soon after the move, Dope Girl Posse broke up.

Eve had to start high school in a place where she had no friends. It was a tough time. Eve was unhappy and it showed.

"I got punished a lot. I got in trouble for cutting school, staying out late, lying about detention, and lying about homework," Eve said. "I hated high school. I always knew there was something else."

Eve's grades began to go down, and she made friends with a rough crowd of kids. Then she met a girl who liked to rap and the two of them performed together. They called themselves EDGP, pronounced "Egypt." The girls stayed out late a lot, and that made Eve's mother mad.

As much as she hated high school, Eve did graduate. With school behind her, she could sing and rap all day.

As much as she hated high school, Eve did graduate. With school behind her, she could sing and rap all day. But with no money and no idea how to make any, the future was scary.

On Her Own

At age 17, Eve gave herself three years to become a star.

She liked EDGP, but she was ready to be on her own and shake things up. She said goodbye to her friend and set out alone.

Calling herself Eve of Destruction, she began to make a name for herself in local clubs. Eve became a very good rapper. She also became known as a talented emcee.

Emcee comes from M.C., short for *master of ceremonies*. An emcee is the person who acts as the host during special occasions. He or she can also be the person who plays the music at dance clubs. An emcee mixes the music together to create a beat.

Eve wrote her raps and often "battled" with other rappers. This kind of battle wasn't a real fight. It was a contest of talent.

Each rapper would take a turn making up a rhyme on the spot. This form of rap is called freestyle. The best rap wins. Eve won a lot. The crowds loved her vibe. Maybe, Eve thought, she might just make it to the top.

Many rappers perform in nightclubs. On many nights when Eve performed, she was out until very late. The next day she would be tired. These late nights were hard on Eve's mother, who wanted to see her daughter come home earlier.

Her mother also didn't like the people Eve was spending time with. It seemed as if they all had no money and no future.

Eve kept staying out late, and her mother kept getting mad about it.

After a few months, nothing had come from all the time Eve had spent performing solo. She wasn't a star yet. Not even close. She felt it was time for a change.

> **Eve became a very good rapper. She also became known as a talented emcee.**

At the start of her career Eve stayed out late at night performing at local clubs, much to her mother's dismay.

To get noticed, Eve decided she had to move where the action was. She packed her bags, said goodbye to her family, and moved to New York City.

Eve settled in a tiny apartment in the Bronx, one of the five boroughs of New York. The others are Manhattan, Staten Island, Queens, and Brooklyn. The Bronx is where some famous people, such as Jennifer Lopez, once lived.

Eve got a job at a local shop. At night she rapped at clubs. There were many late nights when Eve would sit alone in her small apartment and wonder if she had done the right thing by moving to New York. She had few friends, money was tight, and she was working so hard.

Eve felt lonely and lost. Was her dream ever going to come true? Was she fooling herself into thinking she could be a star? Maybe it had been a childish dream. She felt about as far away from stardom as she could get.

Eve was ready to give up.

> *To get noticed, Eve decided she had to move where the action was. She packed her bags and moved to New York City.*

Taking a Chance

*I*t was late at night. Eve was taking a break from working in the dark little bar where she had been hired. *This job has no future,* she thought. She wasn't rapping. She just did odd jobs for the owner because she needed the money. She missed her friends and family. She was ready to go back home to Philadelphia. This life wasn't for her. Eve couldn't have felt worse.

Little did she know that something was about to happen that would change her life forever.

The door to the club opened and in walked a familiar face. It wasn't someone she had ever met before—the face was familiar because it belonged to a famous rap star. Eve had seen him on television and heard him many times on the radio.

Known as Mase, he was well known in the rap world for his work with Sean Combs, otherwise known as Puffy or P. Diddy. He had retired from the music scene to study religion and become a minister. But he was still a legend in the business. He was someone Eve respected and admired.

Mase saw Eve and walked over to her. He asked if they could have a talk.

Of course Eve agreed.

She told Mase of her dreams and how she had moved from her home in Philadelphia to New York to try to make them come true. All she had found was a lonely apartment and jobs that paid little money.

Mase listened to Eve. Then he gave her some advice.

"He talked to me for like two hours," said Eve. "He said you are too smart to be doing this. You wanna rap. You want a career. You need to get away from this."

Mase told Eve not to give up her dream—a dream, he said, she was not going to find in that dark little club.

> **Mase told Eve not to give up her dream—a dream, he said, she was not going to find in that dark little club.**

Eve always likes to "keep it real" even in the company of celebrities and much prefers the company of a few close friends and family.

Eve took Mase's advice to heart. She was going to make it. It was time to take things into her own hands.

That night when Eve got home, she made a plan.

With the help of a few friends, Eve dressed up like a delivery girl and went to the New York offices of Aftermath Entertainment, a company run by the famous rap artist and producer Dr. Dre.

When Eve got to the front door, she was scared, but she went in anyway.

To her surprise, she was able to get past the front desk. She took the elevator to the floor where she would find Michael Lynn, the president of Aftermath Entertainment.

As she got closer, Eve prepared herself for anything.

When the doors opened, she told the secretary out front she had a delivery for Michael Lynn. She was led to his office. Eve was actually about to meet Michael Lynn!

She entered and Lynn looked up. Eve took out the tape player she had been hiding and hit Play.

> *Eve took Mase's advice to heart. She was going to make it. It was time to take things into her own hands.*

> **Just a few months shy of her 18th birthday, Eve was going to L.A. to meet one of the biggest names in rap!**

"I started rapping and he was looking at me like, why is this girl rapping?" said Eve.

But Lynn listened. After a few minutes, though, he cut her off and asked her to leave her phone number, saying he would be in touch.

Eve was then dismissed. As she left the building, she just knew he wasn't going to call.

But Michael Lynn called the very next day. He invited Eve to come to Los Angeles to meet Dr. Dre. Eve could hardly believe it.

Just a few months shy of her 18th birthday, Eve was going to L.A. to meet one of the biggest names in rap!

Hard Work
Pays Off

*E*ve was in the home of Dr. Dre. If only her friends could see her!

"I went to his house and we sat in his studio and I was mesmerized," she says, laughing. "I couldn't talk."

Soon they had a deal. Eve went back to New York, packed her bags, and moved to L.A.

"That next week I was in L.A. living in a two-bedroom condo," she says. "I turned eighteen in L.A."

Dr. Dre wanted to see what Eve could do, so he set her up in a studio and asked her to record a few rap songs. One of the songs was titled "Eve of Destruction." It wound up being used on the sound track of the 1998 film *Bulworth*, starring Warren Beatty and Halle Berry. Some other artists on the sound track included LL Cool J, Public Enemy, and Dr. Dre himself.

Even though everyone agreed that Eve had talent, she was often overlooked.

Even though everyone agreed that Eve had talent, she was often overlooked. After eight months she still didn't have an album in the works, and when her one-year contract expired, Aftermath let her go.

Devastated, she returned home to Philadelphia. But as history shows, this is not where her story ends. In fact, what seemed like an ending was actually just a beginning.

Shortly after returning to Philadelphia, Eve started hanging around with an up-and-coming rap star who went by the name of DMX. DMX spent time with a group of young rappers and producers who called themselves the Ruff Ryders Posse. Eve became friends with everyone in the posse. When she was asked to have a rap battle against one of the members, Drag-On, she astounded everybody by holding her own. They asked her to do it again, so she went up against another Ruff Ryder named Infa-Red. Once again she blew everyone away with her style.

Amazed, the all-male group asked Eve to sign on with them as the first female member of the Ruff Ryder Posse.

Eve's career took off with her number one hit "What Ya'll Want." Her rise to stardom had begun.

In the summer of 1999, Eve recorded a single on a Ruff Ryder CD. The CD, called Ruff Ryders Ryde or Die, Volume One, went to number one on the music charts, and Eve's single, titled "What Y'all Want," was soon in the top ten on the *Billboard* chart.

By the age of 26, Eve had become one of the most important women in rap music.

In September 1999, Eve recorded her first solo album. She called it *Let There Be Eve: Ruff Ryders' First Lady.*

It was a hit, entering the charts at number one. Eve was the very first female rapper to ever enter the charts at the number one slot.

The Ruff Ryders Posse set out on a tour to promote the albums. They played to packed houses. Eve had made the big-time.

Her second album, *Scorpion,* released in 2001, was also a success. One of the singles on the album, "Let Me Blow Ya Mind," which she had recorded with Gwen Stefani, was a crossover success. It was popular with a number of different audiences and won them each a Grammy.

By the age of 26, Eve had become one of the most important women in rap music. She had three platinum albums under her belt, including her 2002 album, *Eve-Olution.* A platinum album is a high honor. It means that the album has sold over one million copies.

Along the way Eve also earned the nickname "Pit Bull in a Skirt," for her resolve to make her life a success story.

Eve and Gwen Stefani, the lead singer of "No Doubt," won a Grammy Award for their duet "Let Me Blow Ya Mind."

> **When Eve thinks about her past, she understands that everything happens for a reason.**

And she didn't stop at music. Eve has appeared in a number of movies, including *Barbershop*; *Barbershop 2: Back in Business*; *The Cookout*; and *The Woodsman*. In 2003 she was offered her own television series called, not surprisingly, Eve. It appears on UPN, and in it she plays a fashion designer looking for love.

That same year, Eve launched her own clothing line, called Fetish by Eve. The collection includes leisure and athletic clothing as well as a variety of other fashions that reflect Eve's personal sense of style. Success has finally come to Eve.

"People just have to keep their heads up," she advises. "It's so hard, especially living in a city with a high crime rate, or drugs everywhere. You have to kind of create your own world. You have to go inside yourself, and just try to stay as positive as you can."

When Eve thinks about her past, she understands that everything happens for a reason. Success in the rap world wasn't easy, but the results made the journey well worth it. And her story is far from over.

DISCOGRAPHY

Albums
2002   *Eve-Olution*
2001   *Scorpion*
1999   *Let There Be Eve: Ruff Ryders' First Lady*

Singles
2004   "Your Love" (with Wyclef Jean)
2003   "Satisfaction"
2002   "Gangsta Lovin'" (with Alicia Keys)
2001   "Let Me Blow Ya Mind" (with Gwen Stefani)
1999   "What Y'all Want"
1998   "Eve of Destruction"

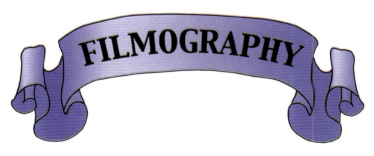

FILMOGRAPHY

2004   *The Woodsman*
        The Cookout
        Barbershop 2: Back in Business
2003   *Charlie's Angels: Full Throttle*
2002   *Barbershop*
        XXX
2000   *Backstage*

CHRONOLOGY

1978	Eve Jihan Jeffers is born November 10 in the rough projects of Philadelphia
1998	Signs one-year deal with Dr. Dre's Aftermath Records; her first musical release, "Eve of Destruction," appears on the *Bulworth* sound track
1999	Joins the Ruff Ryders's camp and her single "What Y'all Want," recorded on the *Ruff Ryders: Ryde or Die*, Volume One album, hit the top ten on the *Billboard* chart; her first album, *Let There Be Eve: Ruff Ryders' First Lady*, hit the charts at number one
2000	Is named Best New Artist at the Source Awards and at the NAACP Image Awards; wins a BET Award for Best Female Hip-Hop Artist; song "Let Me Be" appears in the movie *Nutty Professor II: The Klumps*
2001	Her second album, *Scorpion*, is certified platinum, and "Let Me Blow Ya' Mind," a duet with Gwen Stefani, garners the MTV Video Music Award for Best Female Video
2002	The single "Let Me Blow Ya Mind" wins a Grammy; Eve lands significant roles in the movies *Barbershop* and *XXX*
2003	UPN signs Eve to star in her own television show; Eve unveils her clothing line, Fetish by Eve
2004	Acts in three movies; her duet with Wyclef Jean, "Your Love," appears on the sound track to the movie *50 First Dates*

FOR FURTHER READING

Absolute-Eve.com
     http://www.absolute-eve.com/www/news.htm
Jeannine Amber, "Eve: Blonde Ambition," *Essence*, March 2004.
"Eve," Divastation.com
     http://divastation.com/eve/eve_bio.html
Kris Ex, "Eve: Not Just One of the Guys," *IndieSent Exposure
     Presents: A Hip-Hop/Rap News Clearinghouse*, August 29, 1999.
     http://www.indiesent.com/news/eve.html
Mark Jacobs, "The First Lady, Why Eve Is the New Look of Rap,"
     Paper, January 2001.
Stacie Lynn Wilson, "All About Eve," *Girl Media*, January 2000.
Don Zulaica, "liveDaily Interview: Eve," *liveDaily*, January 18, 2002.
     http://www.livedaily.com/news/4234.html
     http://www.rockonthenet.com/artists-e/eve.htm

INDEX